DAIRY
Is Good For You!

by
Gloria Koster

PEBBLE
a capstone imprint

Published by Pebble, an imprint of Capstone.
1710 Roe Crest Drive,
North Mankato, Minnesota 56003
capstonepub.com

Library of Congress Cataloging-in-Publication Data
Names: Koster, Gloria, author.
Title: Dairy is good for you! / by Gloria Koster.
Description: North Mankato, Minnesota : Pebble, [2023] | Series: Healthy foods | Includes bibliographical references and index. | Audience: Ages 5-8 | Audience: Grades K-1 | Summary: "Yogurt, cheese, and kefir . . . What do these dairy foods have in common? They're all healthy foods! In this Pebble Explore book, explore where dairy foods come from, what nutrition they provide, and how they help form a healthy diet. Filled with fantastic facts, including dairy alternatives, young readers and report writers will be hungry for more"-- Provided by publisher.
Identifiers: LCCN 2022008198 (print) | LCCN 2022008199 (ebook) | ISBN 9781666351248 (hardcover) | ISBN 9781666351309 (paperback) | ISBN 9781666351361 (pdf) | ISBN 9781666351484 (kindle edition)
Subjects: LCSH: Dairy products in human nutrition--Juvenile literature.
Classification: LCC QP144.M54 K67 2023 (print) | LCC QP144.M54 (ebook) | DDC 613.2/77--dc23/eng/20220602
LC record available at https://lccn.loc.gov/2022008198
LC ebook record available at https://lccn.loc.gov/2022008199

Editorial Credits
Editor: Donald Lemke; Designer: Tracy Davies; Media Researcher: Julie De Adder; Production Specialist: Katy LaVigne

Image Credits
Getty Images: FatCamera, 29, Inti St Clair, 5, JGI/Jamie Grill, 20, Jupiterimages, 27, Matt Porteous, 11, Prostock-Studio, 7; Shutterstock: aleks333, 26, Anna Pustynnikova 25, Baksiabat (doodles), cover and throughout, Es75, 4, Evan Lorne, 28, Fortyforks, 12, gpointstudio, 13, Hatchapong Palurtchaivong, 19, Henadzi Kilent, 15, Iraida Bearlala (background), cover and throughout, Leo Morgan, 9, LightField Studios, cover (front), 8, Maurizio Milanesio, 14, New Africa, 18, 22, Pressmaster, 23, StockphotoVideo, 6, Tonelson Productions, 24, XiXinXing, 21; USDA: 17

All internet sites appearing in back matter were available and accurate when this book was sent to press.

TABLE OF CONTENTS

Words in **bold** are defined in the glossary.

WHAT IS DAIRY?

At breakfast, you have milk with your cereal. Lunch is a grilled cheese sandwich. Yogurt is your snack. You finish the day with a tall glass of milk at dinner.

Milk, cheese, and yogurt all belong
to the dairy group. These foods come
from the milk of animals.

An animal that makes milk is a **mammal**. Mothers feed milk to their young.

Humans are mammals. Many human babies get **nutrients** from their mother's milk.

Kittens and other young mammals feed on their mother's milk.

As they grow, people often eat and
drink dairy that comes from other animals.

Most milk comes from cows. It also comes from goats and sheep. Some people get milk from camels and reindeer.

A man in Saudi Arabia milks a camel.

AT THE FACTORY

A farmer milks cows. Then the milk goes to a factory. The milk is cleaned. Sometimes the amount of fat in the milk is changed.

Some milk is full fat. Some is low fat. Some has no fat at all. Milk with no fat is called skim milk.

Some dairy farmers use special machines to milk their cows.

The top layer of milk is cream. People use cream to make sour cream and butter.

butter

Many people love ice cream and pudding. But these foods have lots of fat. Save them for a treat!

Curds are separated from whey.

Cheese and yogurt are healthy foods. To make cheese, milk is separated into two parts. The solid pieces are called **curds**. The liquid part is **whey**. Cheese comes from the curds.

Yogurt is made by adding **bacteria** to milk. These bacteria will not make you sick. These bacteria are good for you!

DAIRY FOR GOOD HEALTH

MyPlate is a guide for healthy meals. Half your plate should have fruits and vegetables. Half should have **protein** foods and grains.

A glass of milk is on the side. Dairy joins the other food groups to keep you healthy.

Dairy has **calcium**. It has **vitamin** D. These nutrients make strong bones and teeth. They help your heart. They are good for muscles and nerves.

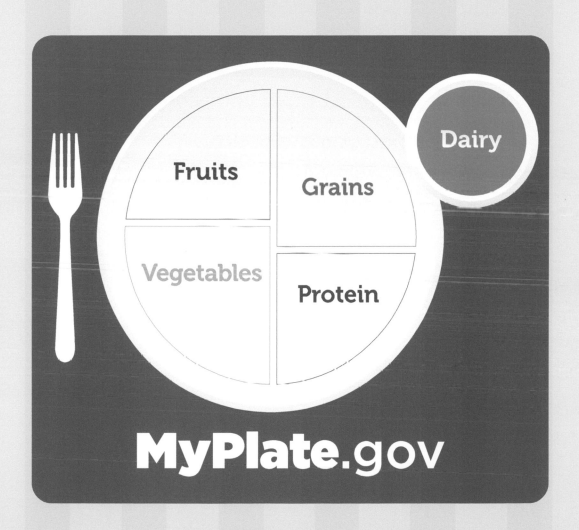

MyPlate.gov

Dairy is important at every age.
It is most important for kids.

Calcium makes bones healthy and strong. You must build your calcium supply when you are young.

Your bones are like a bank. Other parts of your body take out calcium. It is important to put back some calcium every day.

Dairy foods have protein. They have **calories**. These give you energy.

Dairy is a "whole" food. It does not need anything added to it. Dairy is great all by itself!

MAKING SMART CHOICES

Many schools serve lunch. Some schools serve breakfast too. Dairy is a part of healthy school meals.

You can practice healthy eating at home too.

Go shopping with a grown-up. Read food labels. Avoid dairy foods with too much added sugar. Also limit foods with too much fat.

Reading food labels helps you make healthy choices.

Be creative! Try some kefir. This is a yogurt-like drink. People have enjoyed kefir for thousands of years.

Make a low-fat shake or smoothie. Sprinkle cheese on food for flavor. Add some yogurt to fruit.

yogurt with granola and fruit

Not everyone can eat dairy. Milk contains **lactose**. Some people cannot **digest** lactose. They are "lactose intolerant."

Some people drink goat's milk instead of cow's milk. Others drink **beverages** made from rice, almonds, or **soy**. These beverages taste similar to cow's milk.

Soy milk with added calcium is the only plant beverage in the dairy group.

Dairy foods are not the only foods
with calcium. You can get calcium
from nuts and seeds. Leafy green
vegetables have calcium. Beans, **tofu**,
and canned fish do too.

Try to get enough calcium every day. Remember to get lots of exercise too. Walking, running, and climbing are excellent for your bones.

These activities and dairy foods will help keep you healthy and strong!

GLOSSARY

bacteria (back-TEE-ree-uh)—tiny creatures that can live inside the body; some are good and some are bad

beverage (BEV-rij)—a drink

calcium (KAL-see-um)—a mineral found in some foods and needed for strong bones and teeth

calories (KAL-uh-reez)—units of energy

curds (KERDS)—the solid pieces of milk when it is separated to make cheese

digest (dye-JEST)—the process of breaking down foods in the stomach and organs, so it can be used in the body

lactose (LAK-tose)—a sugar found in milk

mammal (MA-muhl)—a warm-blooded animal with a backbone that feeds milk to its young

nutrients (NOO-tree-uhnts)—the parts of food that are needed for growth and health

protein (PRO-teen)—one type of nutrient found in food

soy (SOY)—food that comes from soybeans

tofu (TOE-foo)—a soft food that is made from soy milk

vitamin (VI-tuh-min)—a nutrient in food that works along with minerals to keep us healthy

whey (WAY)—the liquid part of milk when it is separated to make cheese

READ MORE

Schuh, Mari. *Food Is Fuel.* Mankato, MN: Capstone, 2020.

Schwartz, Heather E. *Cookie Monster's Foodie Truck: A Sesame Street Celebration of Food.* Minneapolis: Lerner Publications, 2020.

Webster, Christy. *Follow that Food!* New York: Random House, 2021.

INTERNET SITES

Harvard School of Public Health: "The Nutrition Source"
hsph.harvard.edu/nutritionsource/kids-healthy-eating-plate/

Healthy Kids Association: "Dairy"
healthy-kids.com.au/food-nutrition/5-food-groups/dairy

Let's Eat Healthy: "Milk & Dairy Resources"
healthyeating.org/nutrition-topics/milk-dairy

USDA MyPlate: "Dairy"
myplate.gov/eat-healthy/dairy

INDEX

ABOUT THE AUTHOR

A public and a school librarian, Gloria Koster belongs to the Children's Book Committee of Bank Street College of Education. She enjoys both city and country life, dividing her time between Manhattan and the small town of Pound Ridge, New York. Gloria has three adult children and a bunch of energetic grandkids.